Chill out

Feelings can be tough to manage as kids get older. Sometimes, you might feel a really strong emotion, like anger. Some kids even feel so angry they want to throw things, hit people, or punch a wall. None of these are acceptable behaviors, even though they might seem like normal reactions to feeling angry. This book will help you learn ways to control those feelings, and choose behaviors that communicate them in the healthiest ways.

There are a lot of reasons that kids feel angry. Read the chart below to see how many feelings can be attached to anger.

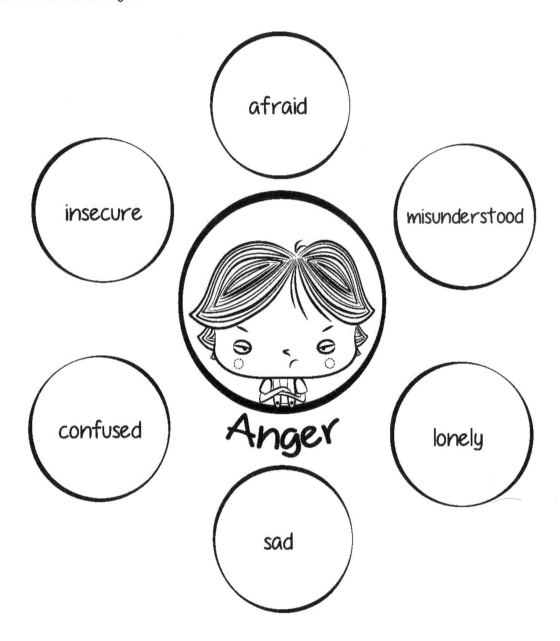

Were there any feelings attached to anger that were not mentioned above? List them below.

_____   _____   _____

_____   _____   _____

What are some things you do when you feel angry?

_____

_____

_____

_____

_____

_____

What are some things you've said when you were angry?

Do you ever let your feelings explode? If so, what effects do your feelings have on yourself and others when they explode? Draw a volcano below, and write your thoughts inside it. Below your drawing, write how these explosive thoughts affect those around you.

The box below contains a list of emotion words. Use some of these words to write a story about a time you got angry on the lines below.

frustrated anxious afraid nervous
lonely intimidated

_____

_____

_____

_____

_____

_____

_____

_____

_____

_____

_____

Illustrate your story in the box below. Make sure you include a picture of yourself, and use one or more of the emotion words you chose in your story in your facial expression.

Draw a picture of something that makes you angry.

How do you chill out? Make a list of things you do to relax when you're feeling stressed out, upset, angry, frustrated, or afraid.

1. _____

2. _____

3. _____

4. _____

5. _____

6. _____

7. _____

8. _____

Draw five balloons below. On each balloon, write or draw something that makes you feel sad, bad, frustrated, or angry.

Now, imagine letting each of the balloons go, one at a time.

One way to chill out is to put your feelings on paper. On the lines below, write a letter to someone who has made you feel angry. Make sure your angry letter is for your eyes only. Then, wait a few days before reading it again, and see if your "thermometer" has changed. Wait until you are good and "chill" before talking to the person you write the letter to. You can write a second draft of the letter to give the person after your thermometer cools.

Dear _____,

_____

_____

_____

_____

_____

_____

_____

_____

From,

_____

Use this page to draft a calm, cool letter about why you were angry. You may send it to the person who made you angry, if you wish.

Dear _____,

_____

_____

_____

_____

_____

_____

_____

_____

_____

From,

_____

Anger and stress affect your body and relationships. On the outline below, mark the places that are affected when you feel angry. Draw an expression on the face, and fill in the thought bubbles with things you think when you're mad.

When you're chilled out, your body probably feels very different. On the outline below, mark the places that are affected when you feel calm. Draw an expression on the face, and fill in the thought bubbles with things you think when you're "chill."

We all need tools to help us stay chill. Most of us have a hammer to bang things out, but few other things to help us deal with our feelings. Draw a toolbox below, and include the tools you have that help you deal with your anger. Examples could be a wrench for adjusting attitude, a screwdriver for turning on soft words, or pliers to pull out bad stuff in a situation. Use your imagination to include your own tools!

Think of the last time you got angry with someone or something. Fill out the chart below to describe the circumstances.

Before I got angry, this happened:	When I got angry, I did this:	After I got angry, my consequence was:

What would you do differently in the middle column? How do you think the consequences would have been different?

_____

_____

Feelings can often be controlled through communication. When you feel upset, voicing why can help you control your thermometer. In each speech bubble below, write a constructive way to communicate your negative feelings.

Controlled breathing is one of the best ways to calm yourself down immediately when you get upset or angry.

Read the poem below, then practice your own breathing to stay cool.

Huff and Puff and Cool Yourself Down!

Sometimes when I get really mad,
I don't know what to do,
I feel my ears get super hot,
and I start to lose my cool;
Mom says one way to keep it,
is to breathe my feelings out;
one long, deep breath through my nose,
reminds me to stay calm;
One slow breath out through my mouth,
and my anger is usually gone!
Sometimes I have to repeat these steps,
until I'm in control.
But every time, it helps me see,
keeping cool is a worthwhile goal.

Everyone feels angry sometimes. Some people get angry more often than others. If you're reading this workbook, you've probably been feeling angry a lot lately. In each of the clouds below, write something that makes you angry.

In the first frame below, draw a picture of yourself feeling happy. In the second frame, draw a picture of yourself feeling angry.

Think about a time when you were really angry. On the lines below, write about what happened that made you angry, as well as how you handled the situation. Include all the details you can remember.

On the lines below, write down everything you've done today. When you finish, use a highlighter to highlight anything that made you feel angry.

1. _____

2. _____

3. _____

4. _____

5. _____

6. _____

7. _____

8. _____

9. _____

10. _____

Below is a web about things that might make someone angry. Fill in the empty spaces with things that make you angry.

Things that make me angry

When I receive a bad grade

There are many different ways to deal with anger. It's a good idea to have a strategy that helps you when you feel yourself getting angry. Below, draw a picture of what you do when you start to feel angry.

It's always a good idea to stop and think before you act — especially if you're angry. Next to each lightning bolt below, write something you might want to say when you're angry. Then, next to the suns, write things you could say instead after you've had time to stop and think.

When we get angry, our hearts fill up with bad thoughts and feelings. In the heart below, draw pictures of things that make you happy. When you start to feel angry, think of your drawing, and try to replace the anger in your heart with these things that make you feel good.

Doing nice things for others can help us feel good and, as a result, keep us from feeling angry. In the stars below, write nice things you could do for others.

Imagine that one of your friends is very angry. They know that they need to calm down, but they don't know what to do. Your friend has asked you for advice. In the space below, write your friend a letter, explaining what you do when you feel very angry.

Dear _____,

_____

_____

_____

_____

_____

_____

_____

_____

_____

_____

From,

_____

Read the paragraph below, and imagine yourself saying the words written there. Then, fill in the lines below.

Sometimes, I get really angry. When I feel myself getting angry, I know I need to find a way to calm down.

Here are some things I do to help myself calm down:

_____

_____

_____

_____

_____

_____

_____

_____

_____

_____

Read each of the sentences below. Then, decide whether each sentence would be a good and productive way to deal with anger. If it would be a good way to deal with your anger, circle the sentence with your favorite color crayon. If it wouldn't be a good way to handle your anger, draw a line through the sentence with your pencil.

1. Hit the person who made you mad.

2. Take a deep breath.

3. Count to 10 before acting.

4. Yell loudly.

5. Talk to your teacher.

6. Ask to speak to the school counselor.

7. Punch a wall.

8. Kick a desk.

9. Write about your feelings in a journal.

10. Say an ugly word.

Draw a picture of a time you felt very angry in the space below, then write a few sentences about why you felt so angry.

_____

_____

_____

_____

Create an acrostic poem about anger below. To complete the poem, think of something that begins with each of the letters in the word that has made you angry in the past. For example, for A, you could use "ARGUING with my brother."

A _____

N _____

G _____

E _____

R _____

Think about a time when a friend or family member made you feel angry. At the top of the page, draw a picture to show what you actually did. At the bottom, draw a picture of what you really wanted to do.

"What I Did When I Was Angry"

"What I Wanted To Do When I Was Angry"

Sometimes people get really angry, and sometimes they get just a little angry. Your own anger level is not the same each time you get angry. Think about the last time you got angry. Were you really angry, pretty angry, or just a little angry? Put a check mark inside the circle that shows how angry you were.

In the face below, draw features to show how your expression looks when you're angry.

Many people who get angry often or easily have a calm-down box. This box contains different items to look at, feel, or even smell that help them calm down. Imagine the box below is your calm-down box. Inside, draw pictures of things that would help you calm down when you're angry. Then, in the spaces below the box, write how each object might help you calm down.

_____

_____

_____

_____

Read each of the following scenarios, and decide how you'd feel if these things happened to you. In the space beside each scenario, write the emotion you think you'd feel. When you finish, go back and circle each time you wrote "angry."

1. You're playing with your best friend on the playground. Another classmate comes up and asks him to play basketball. Your friend runs to the basketball court with your classmate, leaving you behind. How would that make you feel?

2. You're working in class, and your pencil breaks. You ask a classmate if you can borrow a pencil, and she tells you, "No." How would that make you feel?

3. When you walk into class, one of your friends smiles and says hello. How would that make you feel?

4. Your mom and baby sister come to school to eat lunch with you. How would that make you feel?

Did you know there are signs that can let us know we're about to get angry? These might be something like our palms getting sweaty, or our eyes starting to water. Everyone's signals are different, but if you can learn to recognize your own body signals, you may be able to calm yourself before you lose your temper! Think about the things that happen to your body just before your anger gets the best of you. Write them in the boxes below.

Congratulations! You've successfully completed your workbook on dealing with anger. Hopefully the activities you've completed will help you as you're placed in situations that make you uncomfortable and lead to anger. Just remember: When you feel yourself getting angry, stop and use some of the strategies you've written about to calm yourself down. Also, make sure you remember to talk to an adult you trust about how you feel and the things that make you angry.

Congratulations!

_____

has completed this workbook

on this _____ day of _____ in the year _____

Chill Out: A Workbook to Help Kids Learn to Control Their Anger

Text copyright © 2014 by Erainna Winnett, Ed.S.

Book Cover Design copyright © 2014 by Lucia Martinez

www.counselingwithheart.com

ISBN-10: 0615983596

BISAC: Juvenile Nonfiction / Social Issues / Emotions & Feelings

Printed in the United States of America

Made in the USA
San Bernardino, CA
27 January 2018